This book belongs

Paperback ISBN: 978-1-63731-436-4
Hardcover ISBN: 978-1-63731-438-8
eBook ISBN: 978-1-63731-437-1

Printed and bound in the USA.
NinjaLifeHacks.tv

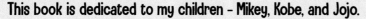

Ninja Life Hacks™

A special thanks to Courtney Fields, Tessa Weigand, Suzette Levy, Janessa LaDawn, and all my readers, young and old, who helped me with this story. Your feedback was priceless.

Consent Ninja

By Mary Nhin

Ninja Life Hacks

There was a time I didn't know I had control of my own body and that I had a voice.

I've summed it up and call it the B.O.S.S. method!

Boundaries

Object (say no!)

Speak up (by saying what you want or how you feel)

Share (with a safe adult or trusted friend)

What's a boundary, anyways?

When we give consent, it means we agree to something, especially when it has to do with our bodies. Consent allows us to be in charge of our bodies and set boundaries, so others know what we like and don't like.

Boundaries are limits. When someone says or does something that trespasses our boundaries, we can **object** by saying no:

(no, not with the dog)

Sometimes, someone you know or a stranger may do things that make you uncomfortable. These things may involve:

No matter what, remember to share with a safe adult or trusted friend, even if the behavior has stopped.

Should you share your friends' private pictures or stories? No!

Imagine a neighbor just asked for a hug. You agreed. But a few seconds later, it doesn't feel right. Can you change your mind? Yes! You can change your mind anytime.

Sometimes, people might get upset at you for changing your mind and that's okay. It's still your body.

Just because someone is wearing certain clothing, it doesn't mean consent either. We can't assume we know why people are dressed a certain way. Maybe they wear that to sleep or they just like wearing it daily...

Remember that no matter what, when someone doesn't respect your boundaries, it's **NEVER** your fault.

If someone doesn't respect your boundaries, it's time to get help:

- Tell a safe adult
- Reach out to childhelphotline.org
- Contact police 9-1-1

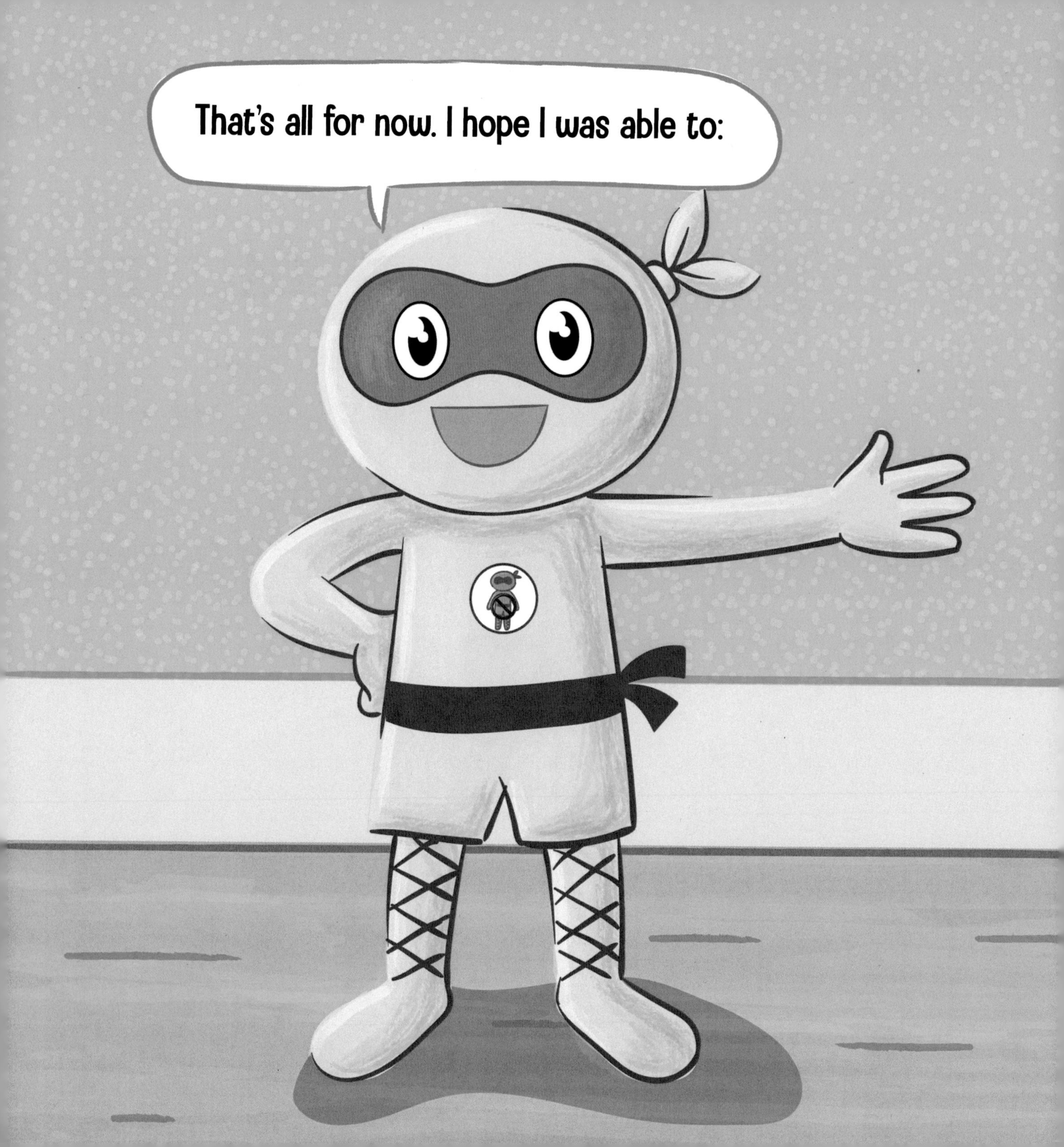
That's all for now. I hope I was able to:

Help you understand and practice consent

Help you recognize and set boundaries

Help you communicate better

Offer ways to get help

Now you know all about consent and the **B.O.S.S.** method!

Boundaries

Object (say no!)

Speak up (by saying what you want or how you feel)

Share (with a safe adult or trusted friend)

I love to hear from my readers. Email me your feedback or thoughts on what my next story should be at growgritpress@gmail.com

Yours truly, Mary

 @marynhin   @GrowGrit
#NinjaLifeHacks

 Ninja Life Hacks

 Mary Nhin   Ninja Life Hacks

 @ninjalifehacks.tv

70541964R00022